Advance F
The RiskA

MW01327381

"*The RiskADay Journal* will change lives." *Susan Wooldridge, Author of poemcrazy: freeing your life with words*

"Laura Biering's sensitivity to the human need for a deep respect and belief in oneself, and her light-hearted wisdom in encouraging the brave acceptance of each challenge with hope and confidence, are uplifting and contagious. This journal of her exploration into the path toward becoming an authentic self is pure gift. She offers a way to engage answers to Mary Oliver's beautiful question, 'What do you plan to do with your one wild and precious life?'" *Janie Cook, Retired Teacher*

"Thinking about and taking a risk a day helps remove the fear of taking risks and helps me to overcome challenges." *Lori Buff, Studio Potter*

"*The RiskADay Journal* provides practical suggestions about how to integrate self-concept, creativity, and risk-taking. The book is all about taking charge of your life and setting goals that lead to self-actualization." *Dr. James S. Taylor, Management Consultant and Distinguished Professor of Communication, Retired*

"This RiskADay concept is brilliant! Especially the notion that even a small intentional risk can have big impact. I like flexing my "risk muscle" daily, which builds up my strength and confidence so that the big scary risks aren't quite so daunting. I highly recommend it!" *Martha Carnahan, Professional Certified Coach*

"I've always been a believer in writing down goals. Whether you put ink to paper or pixel to plasma screen, acknowledging your dreams is the first step in making them happen. But taking a risk a day isn't just a wish list for your future life. It's a transformative way of living intentionally and authentically. I won't lie to you – it takes courage. But the good news is that you can step forward boldly, or in fear and trembling. You can take tiny steps or huge strides. The important thing is that you will be moving forward, toward a better understanding and realization of your true, fulfilled self." *Kory Wells, Software Developer Turned Creative Writer and Performance Poet*

Advance Praise for
The RiskADay Journal

"I find the idea of taking an intentional risk each day daunting but very exciting. I think my life is pretty 'tame.' Certainly risking more would spice it up. This *RiskADay Journal* is just what I need and want." *Mary Ann Taylor, Artist and Retired Banker*

"The whole concept of taking a risk a day brings about a kind of awareness that I don't think I'd have known were it not for participating as a blogger at RiskADay.com. I found out that I take a lot more risks than I thought I did, which boosted my self-esteem immensely. Best of all, it's a way of living that feeds itself – with each risk taken, I am stronger and more capable than before, and that much more willing (and able) to risk again. Contemplating the risk I'll take today makes it even more interesting to get out of bed each morning!" *Suzanne Bird-Harris, Web Developer/Online Business Coach*

"Taking a conscious risk a day, no matter how small, has made me so aware of all the unconscious risks I've been taking all along. It's helping me learn not to be so afraid of the "big" risks and is helping me understand that big risks are just a bunch of tiny risks, taken one at a time." *Janet K. Carter, Senior Marketing Manager*

"*The RiskADay Journal* will change your life, if you let it. I am one of the RiskADay.com bloggers, and it has been useful for me to have a structure (and deadlines) for wrangling with my fears and potential choices, and for putting into words what I am going to do about it. Then, of course, there's the doing it! Participating in this practice on a monthly basis has had a profound effect on me. It has been an excellent source of affirmation, and a great motivator for me to more firmly stand my ground. I can only imagine how powerful it could be to do this for myself on a daily basis. Thanks, Laura, for this great opportunity." *Betsey Brogan, Licensed Massage Therapist*

"Bringing light to the risks I (often unconsciously) take every day, as well as intentionally focusing on taking even more risks, has greatly increased my confidence and joie de vivre!" *Veronica Samoulides, Event Planner*

Advance Praise for
The RiskADay Journal

" Risks can be big or small. The big risks we think of are ones like jumping out of an airplane. However, it is the small risks that we don't think about at all (and don't take) that can cause our lives to stagnate. Laura is a gifted coach, author, and creative goddess who, in her *RiskADay Journal*, skillfully walks readers through the process of taking risks. She helps you to take the risks that really change your life. If you want live your life more fully, this is a must-have!" *BevAnn Bonds, Small Business Owner*

"*The RiskADay Journal* is a comprehensive guide that helps you understand why you should take risks. Moreover, it is a real how-to guide for life." *Tom Vizzini, Business Support Specialist*

The RiskADay
Journal

28 Days
to Being You Out Loud
with
Courage,
Creativity
and
Confidence

For dear Sarah,
Happy Risking!
Laura

by Laura Overstreet Biering, MM, CPCC, PCC

First Edition Printed, 2010

Cover and Interior Layout Design: Vanessa Lowry
Charts and Journal Page Graphics: Kendra Armacost
Cover Photography: Galina Barskaya I Dreamstime.com

Books may be purchased in bulk for educational, business, fundraising or sales promotional use. For information please write:

True Voices, Inc. • 403 W. Ponce de Leon Avenue, Suite 108 • Decatur, GA 30030
Email: laura@truevoices.com

Non-Fiction/Self-Help/Personal Transformation
ISBN 978-1-61005-014-2

Printed in the United States of America

Table of Contents

Remember the Paradox and the Point
Be You Out Loud™/Learn, Love, Live, Lead Chart

Week One: Learn

Week Two: Love

Week Three: Live

Week Four: Lead

Dedications

I dedicate this book with **Gratitude**
for the lives of my grandmothers,
Ora Doris Adams Rosencrance,
Annie Belle Brinson Overstreet
and **Mary Pinckard Bryan Taylor.**

I dedicate this book with **Love** *for the life of my mother,*
Mary Annette Luck Overstreet Taylor.

I dedicate this book with **Hope** *for the lives of my nieces,*
Sarah Ann Overstreet and **Kate Elise Overstreet.**

I dedicate this book with **Joy** *for the life of my partner,*
Martha Jean Carnahan.

I dedicate this book with **Enthusiasm** *for the life of*
YOU.

Be You Out Loud™

Setting the Stage

I've set the stage.
The people will come.
They will listen
And I will, too.
Together we will manifest
Destiny.

The river of creativity
Below the surface, around, within,
Connecting us all
Will flow, is flowing now.
That which swims there is
Endless ~

Endlessly awaiting our imagination and love, a
Velveteen Rabbit
Of sorts. Once given light,
The exchange is mutual.
And the more alive we
Become All.

Ah, the gifts of reciprocity
That come simply
From listening then acting.
My soul whispers.
My spirit acts.
My heart soars.

And yours?

Laura Overstreet Biering ©2009

I've found that luck
is quite predictable.
If you want more luck,
take more chances.

- Brian Tracy

CHAPTER 1: A RiskADay Keeps the Heart in Play

All serious daring starts from within. ~ Eudora Welty

Welcome to My World!

For several years now, I've been taking at least one risk every day, usually pre-planned, and then taking note of the results of my actions. Not only has this practice been extremely rewarding for me professionally, but it has been the most effective tool I've found for building the Courage Muscle, the *heart*. (At the root of the word courage is *couer*, the French word for heart.) This, in turn, has led to greater levels of self-esteem and self-confidence, which, needless to say, has sent my personal "Alive-O-Meter" rankings off the charts!

I am delighted that you have chosen to join me in this endeavor, and I am confident that you, too, will come to love it as much as I have! For me, it has been an enlivening ride of personal growth; full of rich learning and forward motion – in other words, risk *and* reward. Can you see why I so *heartily* recommend it?

As a general rule, we are not taught to take risks. Instead, we are encouraged, by a multitude of well-meaning folks, to take care. I, too, am well-meaning, but I'm encouraging you to *care enough to take risks!* And not just for the heck of it, either. I want you to take risks on purpose, so that you, too, can **Learn** about yourself, **Love** who and whatever it is you find in the learning, **Live** the life that only you can live, and then **Lead** the world, by joyful example, to do the same.

I had such great success with this tool that I began sharing it with my clients, and with astounding results. Finally, a little more than two years ago, I felt it was time to launch the idea to the rest of the world, and I began a blog, www.RiskADay.com.

Even though I was taking a risk each day, it was a challenge to write daily blog posts. Others told me not to worry about it, and to simply write when I could or when I had the urge. Yet I felt that the name of the blog really lent itself to having a new post every day. And still, I didn't make it happen.

The voices in my head bombarded me with judgment and doubt: "Did I have enough to say? Would it be worth reading? Or would people simply think I was being self-indulgent? And would they be right?"

In addition, the to-do lists and other items on my desk stacked up and shouted at me with reminders of things I should be doing instead: "Don't forget to call the printer, the pet sitter, the plumber, your brother. Call this potential client and return the email of that current one. And don't forget to pay that bill, ask that question, write that book, become a star. And, by the way, when are you going to fit in your exercise, your healthy eating, your time with loved ones, time with *yourself*?" Clearly, I had a few things distracting me.

As I discussed this with my friend and Online Business Manager, Suzanne Bird-Harris, she lightly threw out a suggestion that I latched onto for dear life: "Why don't you ask others to write *with* you? You could get enough contributors so that every day is covered." Oh, the relief I felt at the idea of this! In practically no time at all, I was in action around this new plan, and soon, it was up and running!

Enter: The Beautiful Blogging Babes

Now, if you go to www.RiskADay.com, you will see that I have many wise and wonderful contributors keeping the blog nourished with rich and valuable content. My Beautiful Blogging Babes, as I lovingly call them, are posting there, nearly daily! They are writing about the risks they are planning to take, those they have taken, and what they have learned as a result. In other posts, you will see their philosophical musings about risk, what they have come to believe about risking, or where they are in the process of forming their beliefs. In still other posts, the risks taken are evident in the brave openness of the posts themselves. Knowing these women, I am not surprised by their courage. What has been an unexpected and heart-warming outcome, however, is that, as a result of their courageous willingness to share honestly, these Beautiful Blogging Babes have moved from being a diverse group of strangers to a community of support, still diverse, yet unified. And, while each post is a representation of the individual's voice, together they speak of the universal questions we all face, and the efforts we make to embrace them during our time here, gracefully and gratefully.

But what does all this have to do with you?

The Case for You Being You Out Loud™

Our world is like a great big puzzle, and there is a unique space in that puzzle for each and every one of us. There has never been another Laura Luck Overstreet Biering, and there never will be, and the same is true about you. Therefore, we must each do what it takes to fill our own unique spaces, because nobody else ever can or ever will. But how do we do that?

We must be our full, true selves – the magnificent, human, spiritual, multi-faceted, creative, authentic beings that we each were created to be. It is only by being ourselves that we, as individuals, have a chance for rich, fulfilling, joyful lives. And, it follows, that it is only through being ourselves – filling our spaces – that our world has a chance to function at its optimal level. So, being yourself – saying what you think, listening to and then acting upon the whispers from deep within, even honoring those long lost dreams – is not only your right, but also your responsibility! It gives a whole new meaning to the phrase, *Think Globally, Act Locally*, doesn't it?

The model on the next page is a visual representation of the Be You Out Loud™ Philosophy. I won't go into a greatly detailed explanation, but I will point out a few things that apply to this discussion.

As you can see, around the center of the diagram, there are a couple of shapes akin to puzzle pieces. The shape at the base, in the dark magenta hue, is the one that represents each individual's unique space. For our purposes, I'd like you to think of it as *Your Unique Space in the Global Puzzle*.

Now notice that your unique space is at the intersection of (your) Authenticity, (your) Creativity and (your) Divinity. Yes, it's there, where these three birthrights connect – in you – that the potential lies for you to know, love and be all that you were created to be, and to actively contribute that to the rest of the world, all the while leading by example.

The pale purple piece that is on top of the deep magenta shape is representative of the life you are living now. Look carefully – perhaps you're not as far off as you thought! There are several things for you to notice about this piece. One is that it is not as rich in color as that which is representing Your Unique Space. Another is that there is something on the edges of this piece, represented in yellow on this diagram. And last is the fact that this top piece is roughly the same shape as Your Unique Space, only slightly askew and smaller.

Be You Out Loud™

A Visual Representation of the True Voices Philosophy of Claiming Your Space in the World

Affirm Your Beliefs ▶ Acknowledge Your Desire ▶ Utilize Your True Divining Rods™

So, what do you think all of this means? Well, have you heard that the great artist, Michelangelo, said that he didn't carve his masterpiece,

The David, out of the rock? He said that, instead, he simply chipped away what wasn't David, until only David remained. This is what I am suggesting we do. We must know ourselves as the beautiful, magnificent, divine creations that we are, and love ourselves enough to let go of anything that isn't in alignment with that. In essence, we must, little by little, chip away what isn't ourselves, until only we remain. And then we must live our lives, the ones that each of us alone is here to live, calibrating in the direction of our own unique spaces all along the way. Then finally when we carve out our own spaces, we are in the position to stretch into all that we are, and are meant to be.

I realize that this process seems linear, and I am, in fact, presenting it that way. In reality, however, it is more than linear. I am sure you can see that it is also iterative, cyclical, holographic and spiral. And while we are in the process of **Learning, Loving,** and **Living,** we are also creating a ripple out into the world, and **Leading** others, to do the same.

*It's not because
things are difficult
that we dare not venture.
It's because
we dare not venture
that they are difficult.*

- Seneca

CHAPTER 2: What's a Risk, Anyway, and Why Should I Care About Taking One?

I have never seen anyone take a risk for growth that was not rewarded a thousand times over. ~ *John O'Donohue*

Coffee, Mr. Mayor?

Risk-taking is different for everyone. What I consider a risk might be a simple task for you. One of the risks I took last year was to contact the mayor of the City of Decatur, GA, where my office is located. I wanted to take him out for coffee and to learn more about him. He seemed to be such a likeable guy, and I believed him to be a good steward of Decatur. I wanted to know what his dreams were for the city, and for himself, and what challenges might still be in the way of his realizing those dreams. And ultimately, if it seemed right at the time, I wanted to tell him that I'd like to be on his support team, and to ask if he'd consider becoming a client.

For you, this might seem like no big deal. You might already have conversations with mayors, governors or presidents. You may even have some of them as clients or friends. But for me, this was a risk. What made it so? The simple answer is that I was afraid of what might happen. Just not knowing the outcome of some proposed action isn't enough by itself to make that action a risk. For example, there's plenty I don't know about what would happen if I repainted my house the lovely shade of yellow it already is. There might be trouble with the contractor, some damage to the house might be revealed in the process, or the paint brand I prefer might have become exorbitantly expensive since I last purchased it. As unpleasant or inconvenient as those outcomes might be, they don't scare me.

If, for some reason, I wanted to paint my house an uncommon color, such as a blinding orange or a putrid green, for instance, *then* I would be scared. What might my more traditional friends think of this change I'd made? What would the neighbors say? Would they make my life miserable by demanding I change it or move? What if I hate it and I don't have the money to do it over in another color? Now those are scary thoughts, and they show me that, if I really wanted to do that, it would, in fact, be a risk.

As you, yourself, may have experienced, sometimes it seems as though the unknown is scarier than the known, even if you don't particularly like the known that you know! All kinds of additional questions and scary thoughts are born out of not knowing. In the case of my wanting to ask the mayor to join me for coffee, the following questions are some of the ones I found myself asking:

- *What will he think when he gets my message? He doesn't know me "from Adam!" And if he **does** know who I am, what will he think about the fact that I don't even live in Decatur and I want to take up some of his time?*

- *What if he tells other people, and what will they think? Will they think I am crazy? Brazen? Conceited? Will I be asked to cancel my membership in the Decatur Business Association, or worse yet, be simply ignored at all upcoming meetings?*

- *What will **I** think? Will I be sorry I made the call? Embarrassed?*

- *What if he laughs at me? What if he says no?*

- *What if he says yes and then expects too much?*

- *What if he hires me, loves what I do, and then hires me to work with the whole city government and I somehow do a terrible job and I have to close my office and move to another state?*

To you, these "what ifs" may seem extreme. And, given the truth of what actually happened, maybe they were. They were also, however, very real to me and could have kept me from going for what I wanted. But they didn't. And I owe this solely to the fact that I had already been taking my daily risks, building my Courage Muscle, by the time I had the idea about taking the mayor out for coffee.

FYI: I did call the mayor. He did say yes. If he laughed at me or ridiculed me to his friends behind my back, I never found out about it. We had a lovely visit over coffee, I did ask for the business, he said he'd think about it, and I even followed up. We have yet to do any business together, but I cannot say that nothing has come of my taking that risk. For one thing, the Mayor of Decatur, GA knows who I am, and when we see each other in town, or at that local coffee shop, we always wave or exchange a smile. Also, who knows what business might eventually come of our having that conversation? I certainly don't. But neither of those is the biggest thing I got from taking that risk. I got a higher confidence level, more self-esteem, and my Courage Muscle, my heart, is stronger for having taken it, regardless of the eventual outcome. And, I am even better prepared for further risking. Who knows, maybe I'll ask the President of the United States to join me for coffee next!

The Fire of Desire

Sometime after the exercise of building my Courage Muscle by asking the mayor out for coffee, it became clear that a long-standing dream of mine wasn't going away. I really wanted to create and perform a one-woman show. I wanted this so much that, in spite of my attempts to squelch this burning desire inside me, it only continued to grow! It felt as though it wasn't just little ol' me who wanted this. Strangely enough, it felt that my soul and spirit wanted it, too.

As I am sure you already know, having a desire this deep (and wide and high), without taking action toward meeting it, grows quite painful. And that is where I had been too long – in pain. Finally, I decided that I was the only one who could make this pain go away, and that, as far as I could see, it would only go away in one of two ways. I could either (1) figure out how to genuinely give up the desire, or (2) do some serious risking. Not willing to give up on my dream – risking it was. Good thing I'd been working my Courage Muscle.

Of course there were voices of fear in my head, more than I could count. But once I realized how deep the desire was, and that I was the only one who could take charge of fulfilling it, I took to action.

In the span of a few hours, I set the date, secured a performance space, created and sent out invitations. After taking those first few risks, there was little room for turning back. Sure, I could have, but truly, I didn't want to turn back – just the opposite, in fact! By taking those four little actions, one after another, feelings of excitement followed. Here I was on the precipice of actually following through on experiencing this dream. I was elated! (Warning – risk can do that!)

Of course, there were new choices, decisions and actions – risks.

As I contemplated the array of potential next moves, necessary ones for making my dream a reality, some of the excitement (actually, a lot of it) waned. Frankly, the idea of crafting a script, and then rehearsing it, rehearsing it some more, and then rehearsing it even more, made me want to crawl under a rock somewhere, never to be heard from again. "But that's the way it's done," one of the (not so) helpful voices said.

Then I remembered Anne Lamott, and her wonderful book, *Bird by Bird: Some Instructions on Writing and Life*. In one of the early chapters, she tells her readers that the way to end up with good writing is to start by allowing yourself to do really bad writing. She also reminds us that the way to learn how to do something is to do it. Right then and there, upon recalling her wisdom, I decided that I wouldn't write a script, and I wouldn't rehearse, either. No! On the day of the show, I would show up at the venue, as would my audience, and right there in front of them, I would create and perform what Anne Lamott would call my "Shitty First Draft!" (A little side note here: The poem at the very beginning of this book, *Setting the Stage*, is one I wrote while contemplating the whole experience of my show.)

This decision brought with it a new set of worries, voices, and risks to consider. But I didn't care. The freedom I felt from figuring out a way I could enjoy this process (and the end product) sent me flying.

FYI: Come the day of the show, fly I did! I had a blast. It was over way too soon. People were moved, shocked, inspired and engaged in the process of assisting me with the next version. In a Q & A session afterward, I received so much good feedback that, once I captured it all, I put it away in a box for safekeeping. And one day, I'll open that box, and get busy with creating what perhaps I'll call my "Crappy Second Draft."

Take a Risk. Get a Reward. Always.

Before you start arguing with me about the title of this section, let me say a thing or two. I know that sometimes we don't get the outcome we had hoped for when taking risks, no matter how much we want it. Sometimes the result is better! And sure, sometimes it's "worse." But I put that in quotation marks because, even though the result can prove to be less than I had hoped for, I am always rewarded from having taken the risk. What I mean is that when I am willing to receive the lesson that simply taking the risk has brought me, regardless of outcome, I learn more about myself, my abilities, my limits and my dreams. I also learn about the reliability of my process of discernment and the strength of my current support systems. I become clearer about what my next steps could be, and how I might go about taking them. And, perhaps most important, I have the glorious experience of being accountable to myself, of being on my own side, and of giving myself a chance to expand my life, as opposed to allowing it to atrophy or stagnate, a fate I would not wish on anyone. And don't we owe it to ourselves to be as fully alive as we can be while we are here, *alive?* I say an unequivocal "yes!"

By the way, I learned all of this only to the extent that I allowed myself to first feel my feelings about not getting what I wanted (but that's for a different book).

Take a look at the following diagram:

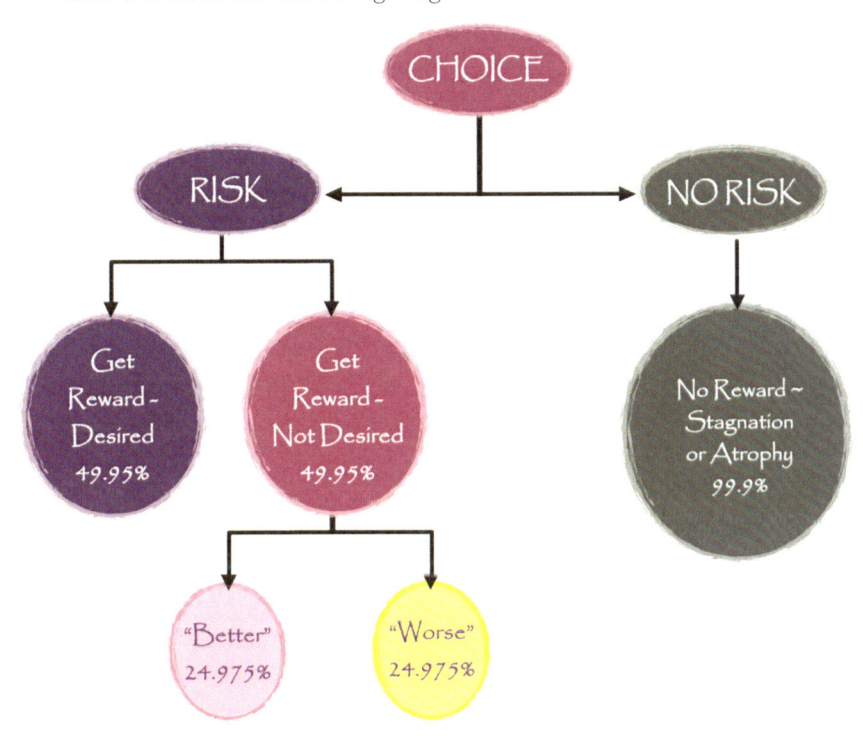

As you can see, you can certainly take *no* risk and have practically no chance of getting what you want. Or you can take a risk, and either get what you want, get something worse or get something better. I'd say those odds are better than taking no risk at all, wouldn't you? Erica Jong would. She said, "If you don't risk anything, you risk even more!"

And, if you need just a little more evidence, check out what the wise Johann Wolfgang von Goethe had to say about it: "The dangers of life are infinite, and among them is safety."

I'm Not Talking Foolishness

Not only do we owe it to ourselves to intentionally take these daily risks for the sake of better lives, but we also owe it to ourselves *not* to take risks before doing our due diligence, and staying in touch with ourselves, calibrating all along the way.

When crossing the street, for instance, whether or not we are at a crosswalk, we are best served by first looking both ways. And if there is a vehicle coming, we are well-taught to take into account how quickly it's moving, whether or not it has a turn signal on, and how fast we know ourselves to be at that moment in time. This is what I am suggesting we do when considering risks. There is an internal process I suggest you use when at a crossroads or faced with a decision. This process can take weeks, a day, a few hours or just moments, depending on the person and the weight of the decision at hand. I call this process the *Due Diligence of Discernment*™, and these are the steps:

1. Introspection
2. Intuition
3. Inspiration
4. Intention
5. Attention
6. Enthusiasm
7. Commitment
8. Courage
9. Confidence
10. Risk
11. Reward
12. Integration

Even though this process moves from the inside, out into action, and then inside again, it is also important to note that, as these steps are being taken, a heightened awareness of what is being experienced and revealed all along the way must also be taken into consideration. It is only with this **consistent, acute calibration** that we can be sure we are taking risks that are aligned with who we are, where we want to go, and why we want to go there.

Another thing to note, once again, is that although the steps are represented here in a linear fashion, and that's the way I recommend that you work with them at first, they won't always have to be taken in such a structured sequence. There will come a time when you are so familiar with them that you'll know where to begin and how to best use them to focus on the decision at hand.

Checking Your Motives
While Choosing Your Risks

I had the opportunity to see an amazing play, a one-woman show called *Jodie's Body*. It was about many things but primarily, it made the assertion that if something as horrible as apartheid could end as the result of *just talking* then surely we could end the war on our bodies. It was powerful and mind-bending, indeed. And, the majority of the play was performed, by Aviva Jane Carlin, also the playwright, in the nude!

Ms. Carlin was not a small woman, neither in frame nor flesh. Nor was she small on the courage scale. She stood on that stage, with all eyes on her, posing and moving about as called for by the script, without an inkling of fear or shame. What a risk! Why on Earth would she choose to do that???

When asked how she was able to do that, she admitted that, at first, it was indeed scary, but she had a message to deliver, so she proceeded. Then, soon after the lights came up, the night of that first performance – in all her glory – she had a realization. Not only was she the most vulnerable person in the room at the moment, she was also the most powerful and the most equipped to deliver this message!

This blew me away. I began to think more about the relationship between vulnerability and authentic, personal power and to see them as two sides of the same coin, inextricably linked. Truly, personal power cannot exist without some level of authentic vulnerability, nor can we be safely vulnerable without also being in touch with our authentic personal power.

I'm sure you see that the risks I am suggesting you take are not those of the "bungee jumping" variety, although if you enjoy that kind of risk and can do it safely, then go right ahead. I am not here to stop you. What I am suggesting, though, is that you take risks that are in service of something. Some of the things I take risks in service of are: love, growth, learning, my health, my "causes," my business, as well for delight and enjoyment.

You get the picture. Just make sure your motives are coming from that place of experiencing and claiming authentic personal power, as opposed to "power over" or "powering through." And if you don't, be forewarned, you may be putting yourself at risk in a way that is dangerous or far more than you bargained for.

Choosing Life

Last year, I had the opportunity to go skydiving with a group of friends in honor of our high school reunion. Having experienced different levels of acrophobia, I had never wanted to skydive before. But something about this offer really called to me. Just thinking about it increased my adrenaline level, and I honestly considered it.

I called my dear coach, Jeanine Mancusi. Knowing that she would support me no matter what, I felt free to fully explore my motives. As it turned out, I wanted to SAY I had been skydiving (to my high school buddies and prospective clients) way more that I actually wanted to do it. But, you know, that urge was still very strong, even though I knew my motive wasn't pure.

"What if I did it anyway? How bad could it be – really?" I posed my questions to Jeanine. "I mean, if I don't have a heart attack from the sheer fear of jumping out of the plane, it could be pretty cool, right? And I'll be doing it in tandem with an expert, so really, what's the worst thing that could happen? A broken limb? I mean, no one ever dies from skydiving, right?"

There was silence on the other end of the phone line. "Jeanine?"

Then she told me. Just a few days before that very call, the husband of a friend of hers, a professional skydiver, had died during a dive because his chute didn't open.

That did it for me. Right then and there I said "no" to skydiving.

I realized that I valued my life more than what others thought of me. That was so cool! But I still had this niggling feeling of shame. I thought to myself, "Here I am, the RiskADay coach, and I'm not willing to take one of the biggest risks of all?" (I can lay it on myself thick sometimes!)

Then I had another conversation with a dear friend I've known since college, Rita Balzotti. She gently reminded me that I take emotional risks every day – risks of the heart. I allow myself to hope and dream and take action toward those dreams. I speak my truth even when it's unpopular and/or it turns my life upside down.

Oh, yeah! She was right. (Having people around who can help you sort out what's real can be a valuable resource, for sure.)

The risks of the heart – these are the ones I fear *and* enjoy. They are the ones that help me to stretch and grow, and they connect me to myself, to others, my world, and to the spiritual realm. And, quite frankly, these are also the ones that not only haven't killed me yet, but bring me alive like no others and allow me to do my part in filling the Global Puzzle.

I am elated that you are embarking on this RiskADay journey with me, and joining me in living and being alive in this way. And I hope that you will let me know of your experience. In fact, I can't wait to hear from you!

Do what you fear
and your fear will die.

- Ralph Waldo Emerson

CHAPTER 3: OK, So What Do I Do Now?

Ultimately we know deeply that the other side of every fear is freedom. ~ Marilyn Ferguson

Start Right Where You Are, Right Now

I have purposefully designed this journal in such a way that you don't have to wait until the first of some given year or month or even the first day of the week to get started. Even if, as you are reading this, the day is almost over, you can still start today! The point is for you just to start. Even if it's scary, even if you think you don't understand well enough, even if you _____!

(You fill in the blank.)

After all, what better day is there to start Learning, Loving, Living and Leading than right here, right now – today?

Make a Commitment

Are you ready yet to give yourself this gift? I am sure you know how important commitment is, so I won't lecture. I will, however, share with you again some of the wise words of Goethe. He said, "Until one is committed, there is hesitancy, the chance to draw back, always ineffectiveness. Concerning all acts of initiative and creation there is one elementary truth, the ignorance of which kills countless ideas and splendid plans: that the moment one definitely commits oneself, then Providence moves, too. All sorts of things occur to help one that would never otherwise have occurred. A whole stream of events issue from the decision, raising in one's favor all manner of unforeseen incidents and meetings and material assistance, which no man could have dreamed would have come his way. Whatever you can do or dream you can do, begin it. Boldness has a genius, power and magic in it."

Convincing argument, eh?

You are Not Alone

Even though this is the last section for now, it is definitely *not* the least. Remember that you have so much support in the world, both seen and unseen.

I know that there are people around you whom you can turn to – friends, a coach, your Higher Self, me, all of the above! On each of the 28 days represented in the journal, there are quotes to prompt and encourage you. Use them as mantras, if you like, as you are approaching your intended risk for the day – or any risk for that matter.

And I, too, will be with you on the journey, continuing to take my risks, building my Courage Muscle, heightening my confidence level, raising my self-esteem, and creating a reality that rocks! And so will the Beautiful Blogging Babes over at RiskADay.com. Don't forget them. Let them support you, too.

Before you know it, a mere 28 days from now, you will have amassed the evidence that you are a strong, brave, creative and powerful person of integrity, and that you can indeed trust yourself. Oh, what a feeling!

And, if you'd like some ideas about possible risks you could take, some company on the journey, or even some proof that I know what I am talking about, you might want to take a look at Appendix I for a list of some of the risks I've taken. Remember that, as mentioned, what constitutes a risk is different for each person, and be assured that, at the time and place of each of these risks, they were, in fact, risks for me.

Remember the Paradox and the Point

There are just a few more things I want to say before I send you off for 4 weeks of risks and rewards.

Yes, you will be focusing on taking at least one intentional risk per day for the next 28 days. Who knows, on some days, you may take the risk of just being open to what risk you will take! And yes, as I have said, this is a seemingly linear path. The paradox is that although that is true, it is also true that while you are working through each section, you will also be gaining ground in each of the others. For instance, you cannot be Learning without Loving yourself enough to do so, Living your life, and Leading those around you. When you are in the Love week, you cannot help but also be Learning, Living and Leading, and so on. I point this out, not to overwhelm you, but to remind you to be aware of it, for it is this kind of awareness that you will find increasingly helpful as you move toward having more of *you* in your life, toward Being You Out Loud™.

This brings me to the most important thing I'd like for you to remember, always: It is your right and your responsibility to Be You Out Loud™, in all the rich layers of what that means. Below is a chart that might assist you with "getting your head around" some of the aspects of this undertaking. Feel free to spend lots of time with it, questioning it, agreeing with it and disagreeing, too, if that feels right. But more than doing what it takes to understand it, I hope you will allow the wisest part of yourself to get your heart, soul and spirit aligned with it, and let it inform you as you move closer and closer to claiming *Your Unique Space in the Global Puzzle*.

BE YOU OUT LOUD™

Learn	Love	Live	Lead
Accept Discover Acknowledge Distinguish	**Own** Embrace Respond Nurture	**Act** Permit (Self) Stand & Stretch Commit	**Actualize** Permit (Others) Intend Claim
Your **Emotions**	Your **Choice**	Your **Beliefs**	Your **Wisdom**
Your **Humanity**	Your **Divinity**	Your **Authenticity**	Your **Creativity**
Your **Values**	Your **Value**	Your **Power**	Your **Impact**
Your **Needs**	Your **Preferences**	Your **Passions**	Your **Compassion**
Your **Happiness**	Your **Joy**	Your **Ecstasy**	Your **Connection**
You as Individual Parts – Your Internal Voices, a Cacophony	**You** as a Whole with Distinct Boundaries, Limits – Your Internal Voices, Chorus & Conductor	**You** as Unique – Your True Voice, a Clear, Soaring Solo	**You** as One with all that Is, Limitless – Your True Voice, Harmonizing with the Global Chorus

Risk

My teacher says,
You've got to stink first.
I tell her, I don't have time to stink -
at 64 years old
I go directly to perfection
or I go nowhere.

Perfection is nowhere,
she says, **So stink.**
Stink like a beginner,
stink like decaying flesh,
old blood,
cold sweat,
she says,
I know a woman who's eighty-six,
last year she learned to dive.

©Lisa Colt, gratefully used with permission from the author

Safe is risky.

~ Seth Godin

CHAPTER 4: # The Journal: Go For It!!!

Week One: Learn

Education is not preparation for life; education is life itself. ~ John Dewey

In this first week, I suggest that you keep in mind the **Learning** aspect of taking at least one risk per day. Some say this is the greatest reward from any risk we take: the learning about ourselves. In order to help you get started on this, below (and during each subsequent week) there are a several questions for you to ponder. I hope that they help you decide just what the perfect risks are for you to take! If not, take whatever risk you can think of. It'll still work its magic, I promise.

Here are this week's questions to ponder:

- *What did you like to do as a child? What did you want to be when you grew up?*

- *What do you like to do now?*

- *When was the last time you did something just for the fun of it?*

- *What do you detest? What is something about which you are enthusiastic?*

- *What emotions are you experiencing right now? And now? And now?*

- *What emotion(s) do you try to avoid "like the plague?"*

- *What is at your core? Who are you, really?*

- *What's your relationship with perfection? What about control? What's the worst that could happen if you let those go?*

- *How do you feel about adventure? What's an adventure you've wanted to try, but haven't yet?*

- *What voices of yours have you silenced along the way? What do they have to say now?*

- *When was the last time you met your own needs?*

- *What roles do you play in your life?*

- *Which roles do you want to hang on to? Which would you rather let go of?*

- *What do you like most about being human?*

Take a moment now to jot down any thoughts or ideas you'd like to capture here, and then dive on in. The water's fine!

_____

_____

_____

_____

_____

_____

_____

_____

_____

_____

_____

_____

_____

_____

_____

_____

_____

_____

_____

It is only in adventure that some people succeed in knowing themselves.
~Andre Gide

Be You Out Loud.

The risk I intend to take today is:

_____

_____

_____

_____

_____

_____

_____

The reason I will take this risk is:

_____

_____

_____

_____

_____

_____

_____

_____

_____

L E A R N

❏ I did it!   ❏ I didn't do it.

The rewards and/or lessons I received from taking (or not taking) the risk are:

_____

_____

_____

_____

_____

_____

_____

_____

_____

_____

_____

_____

_____

_____

_____

_____

_____

_____

_____

_____

_____

The most important thing to remember is this: to be ready at any moment to give up what you are for what you might become.
~W.E.B. Du Bois

We all experience doubts and fears as we approach new challenges. The fear diminishes with the confidence that comes from experience and faith. Sometimes you just have to go for it and see what happens. Jumping into the battle does not guarantee victory, but being afraid to try guarantees defeat. ~ Brian Goodell

2

Be You Out Loud.

LEARN

The risk I intend to take today is:

_____

_____

_____

_____

_____

_____

The reason I will take this risk is:

_____

_____

_____

_____

_____

_____

_____

_____

_____

❑ I did it!   ❑ I didn't do it.

The rewards and/or lessons I received from taking (or not taking) the risk are:

_____

_____

_____

_____

_____

_____

_____

_____

_____

_____

_____

_____

_____

_____

_____

_____

_____

_____

_____

_____

_____

_____

_____

_____

_____

_____

_____

_____

_____

_____

_____

_____

_____

_____

_____

_____

_____

_____

_____

_____

_____

_____

_____

_____

_____

_____

_____

_____

_____

I learn by going where I have to go.

~ Theodore Roethke

We learn to do something by doing it. There is no other way. ~ John Holt

Be You Out Loud.

The risk I intend to take today is:

_____

_____

_____

_____

_____

_____

The reason I will take this risk is:

_____

_____

_____

_____

_____

_____

_____

_____

_____

LEARN

❑ I did it!   ❑ I didn't do it.

The rewards and/or lessons I received from taking (or not taking) the risk are:

_____

_____

_____

_____

_____

_____

_____

_____

_____

_____

_____

_____

_____

_____

_____

_____

_____

_____

_____

_____

_____

One hundred percent of the shots you don't take don't go in. ~ Wayne Gretzky

A man would do nothing, if he waited until he could do it so well that no one would find fault with what he has done. ~ Cardinal Newman

Be You Out Loud.

The risk I intend to take today is:

_____

_____

_____

_____

_____

_____

The reason I will take this risk is:

_____

_____

_____

_____

_____

_____

_____

_____

_____

_____

❑ I did it!   ❑ I didn't do it.

The rewards and/or lessons I received from taking (or not taking) the risk are:

_____

_____

_____

_____

_____

_____

_____

_____

_____

_____

_____

_____

_____

_____

_____

_____

_____

_____

_____

_____

_____

_____

_____

_____

_____

_____

_____

_____

_____

_____

_____

_____

_____

_____

_____

_____

_____

_____

_____

_____

_____

_____

_____

_____

_____

_____

_____

Progress always involves risk;
you can't steal second with your foot on first.

~ Frederick Wilcox

One of the greatest discoveries a man makes, one of his great surprises, is to find he can do what he was afraid he couldn't do. ~ Henry Ford

Be You Out Loud.

L E A R N

The risk I intend to take today is:

_____

_____

_____

_____

_____

_____

The reason I will take this risk is:

_____

_____

_____

_____

_____

_____

_____

_____

❑ I did it!   ❑ I didn't do it!

The rewards and/or lessons I received from taking the risk (or not):

_____

_____

_____

_____

_____

_____

_____

_____

_____

_____

_____

_____

_____

_____

_____

_____

_____

_____

_____

_____

_____

_____

_____

We find out about ourselves only when we take risks.
~ Magdalena Abakanowicz

Man can learn nothing except by going from the known to the unknown.

~ Claude Bernard

Be You Out Loud.

The risk I intend to take today is:

_____

_____

_____

_____

_____

_____

The reason I will take this risk is:

_____

_____

_____

_____

_____

_____

_____

_____

_____

_____

❑ I did it!   ❑ I didn't do it.

The rewards and/or lessons I received from taking (or not taking) the risk are:

_____

_____

_____

_____

_____

_____

_____

_____

_____

_____

_____

_____

_____

_____

_____

_____

_____

_____

_____

_____

_____
_____
_____
_____
_____
_____
_____
_____
_____
_____
_____
_____
_____
_____
_____
_____
_____
_____
_____
_____
_____
_____
_____

I am always doing that which I cannot do, in order that I may learn how to do it. ~ Pablo Picasso

He has not learned the lesson of life who does not every day surmount a fear.

~ *Ralph Waldo Emerson*

Be You Out Loud.

The risk I intend to take today is:

_____

_____

_____

_____

_____

_____

_____

The reason I will take this risk is:

_____

_____

_____

_____

_____

_____

_____

_____

_____

LEARN

❑ I did it!   ❑ I didn't do it.

The rewards and/or lessons I received from taking (or not taking) the risk are:

_____

_____

_____

_____

_____

_____

_____

_____

_____

_____

_____

_____

_____

_____

_____

_____

_____

_____

_____

_____

_____

_____

Only those who will risk going too far can possibly find out how far one can go. ~ T.S. Eliot

Week Two: Love

And the day came when the risk it took
to remain tight in a bud was more painful
than the risk it took to blossom. ~ Anaïs Nin

Congratulations – you are well on your way now. No matter how long it took you to get through the first seven "days," you are here and **Loving** yourself by moving forward!

Here are this week's questions to ponder:

- *What's the most loving thing you can do for yourself today?*

- *What action(s) have you been worrying about or procrastinating on taking?*

- *What's your relationship with disappointing others? What about with disappointing yourself?*

- *Is there someone you love who might like to be reminded of that love?*

- *When was the last time you looked in the mirror and said "I love you" to yourself?*

- *What random (or not so random) act of kindness are you willing to perform today?*

- *What's a truth you haven't yet admitted to yourself?*

- *In what areas of your life are you conforming or boxing yourself in, and why? Is that painful?*

- *Which do you prefer: vanilla or chocolate (or both), orange or blue, aerobics or yoga? When was the last time you asked for what you preferred?*

- *Have you embraced your value as a spiritual being having a human experience?*

- *Do you treat yourself as a precious object? Is where you live a sanctuary, an oasis, a home?*

- *How often do you allow yourself to be spontaneous, open to what might be revealed?*

- *What boundaries need to be set and honored?*

- *What's the thing you love most about your life? What do you love most about yourself?*

- *How aligned are you with the choices you are currently making in your life?*

- *What is within you aching to be brought forth?*

Take a moment now to jot down any thoughts or ideas you'd like to capture here, and then dive on in. The water's fine!

You may be disappointed if you fail, but you are doomed if you don't try. ~ Beverly Sills

Be You Out Loud.

LOVE

The risk I intend to take today is:

_____

_____

_____

_____

_____

_____

The reason I will take this risk is:

_____

_____

_____

_____

_____

_____

_____

_____

_____

❑ I did it!   ❑ I didn't do it.

The rewards and/or lessons I received from taking (or not taking) the risk are:

_____

_____

_____

_____

_____

_____

_____

_____

_____

_____

_____

_____

_____

_____

_____

_____

_____

_____

_____

_____

_____

_____

_____

_____

_____

_____

_____

_____

_____

_____

_____

_____

_____

_____

_____

_____

_____

_____

_____

_____

_____

_____

_____

We will discover the nature of our particular genius when we stop trying to conform to our own or to other people's models, learn to be ourselves, and allow our natural channels to open.
~ Shakti Gawain

Only by learning to live in harmony with your contradictions can you keep it all afloat. ~ Audre Lorde

Be You Out Loud.

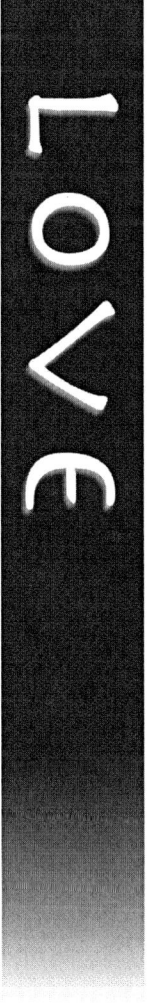

The risk I intend to take today is:

_____

_____

_____

_____

_____

_____

The reason I will take this risk is:

_____

_____

_____

_____

_____

_____

_____

_____

❑ I did it!   ❑ I didn't do it.

The rewards and/or lessons I received from taking (or not taking) the risk are:

_____

_____

_____

_____

_____

_____

_____

_____

_____

_____

_____

_____

_____

_____

_____

_____

_____

_____

_____

_____

_____

_____

_____

_____

_____

_____

_____

_____

_____

_____

_____

_____

_____

_____

_____

_____

_____

_____

_____

_____

_____

_____

Once we believe in ourselves, we can risk curiosity, wonder, spontaneous delight, or any experience that reveals the human spirit. ~ e e cummings

Action may not always bring happiness;
but there is no happiness without action.

~ Benjamin Disraeli

Be You Out Loud.

The risk I intend to take today is:

_____

_____

_____

_____

_____

_____

The reason I will take this risk is:

_____

_____

_____

_____

_____

_____

_____

_____

_____

❏ I did it!   ❏ I didn't do it.

The rewards and/or lessons I received from taking (or not taking) the risk are:

_____

_____

_____

_____

_____

_____

_____

_____

_____

_____

_____

_____

_____

_____

_____

_____

_____

_____

_____

_____

_____

_____

If you bring forth what is within you, what you bring forth will save you. If you do not bring forth what is within you, what you do not bring forth will destroy you. ~ Jesus of Nazareth

*You get in life what you have the courage
to ask for.* ~ Oprah Winfrey

Be You Out Loud.

The risk I intend to take today is:

_____

_____

_____

_____

_____

_____

The reason I will take this risk is:

_____

_____

_____

_____

_____

_____

_____

_____

_____

❑ I did it!   ❑ I didn't do it.

The rewards and/or lessons I received from taking (or not taking) the risk are:

_____

_____

_____

_____

_____

_____

_____

_____

_____

_____

_____

_____

_____

_____

_____

_____

_____

_____

_____

_____

_____

_____

_____

_____

_____

_____

_____

_____

_____

_____

_____

_____

_____

_____

_____

_____

_____

_____

_____

_____

_____

_____

_____

We cannot escape fear. We can only transform it into a companion that accompanies us on all our exciting adventures. ~ Susan Jeffers

Pearls don't lie on the seashore.
If you want one, you must dive for it.
~ Chinese Proverb

Be You Out Loud.

LOVE

The risk I intend to take today is:

_____

_____

_____

_____

_____

_____

The reason I will take this risk is:

_____

_____

_____

_____

_____

_____

_____

_____

❑ I did it!   ❑ I didn't do it.

The rewards and/or lessons I received from taking (or not taking) the risk are:

_____

_____

_____

_____

_____

_____

_____

_____

_____

_____

_____

_____

_____

_____

_____

_____

_____

_____

_____

_____

_____

_____

_____

_____

_____

_____

_____

_____

_____

_____

_____

_____

_____

_____

_____

_____

_____

_____

_____

_____

_____

_____

_____

Healing may not be so much about getting better, as about letting go of everything that isn't you – all of the expectations, all of the beliefs – and becoming who you are. ~ Rachel Naomi Remen

*Never let the odds keep you from doing what
you know in your heart you were meant to do.*
~ H. Jackson Brown, Jr.

Be You Out Loud.

The risk I intend to take today is:

_____

_____

_____

_____

_____

_____

_____

The reason I will take this risk is:

_____

_____

_____

_____

_____

_____

_____

_____

_____

❑ I did it!   ❑ I didn't do it.

The rewards and/or lessons I received from taking (or not taking) the risk are:

_____

_____

_____

_____

_____

_____

_____

_____

_____

_____

_____

_____

_____

_____

_____

_____

_____

_____

_____

_____

_____

_____

_____

_____

_____

_____

_____

_____

_____

_____

_____

_____

_____

_____

_____

_____

_____

_____

_____

_____

_____

_____

_____

The stories of past courage… can offer hope, they can provide inspiration. But they cannot supply courage itself. For this each man must look into his own soul. ~ John F. Kennedy

Do what you can, with what you have, where you are. ~ Theodore Roosevelt

14

Be You Out Loud.

LOVE

The risk I intend to take today is:

_____

_____

_____

_____

_____

_____

The reason I will take this risk is:

_____

_____

_____

_____

_____

_____

_____

_____

_____

❏ I did it!   ❏ I didn't do it.

The rewards and/or lessons I received from taking (or not taking) the risk are:

_____

_____

_____

_____

_____

_____

_____

_____

_____

_____

_____

_____

_____

_____

_____

_____

_____

_____

_____

_____

_____

_____

_____

_____

_____

_____

_____

_____

_____

_____

_____

_____

_____

_____

_____

_____

_____

_____

_____

_____

_____

_____

_____

Every time you don't follow your inner guidance, you feel a loss of energy, loss of power, a sense of spiritual deadness. ~ Shakti Gawain

Week Three: Live

Don't ask yourself what the world needs – ask yourself what makes you come alive, and then go do it. Because what the world needs are people who have come alive. ~ Harold Thurman

Wow – you're halfway through – congratulations! How are you feeling about your progress? How's that Courage Muscle doing? No matter what, remember your commitment, keep on going and **Live**!

Here are this week's questions to ponder:

- *What is different about you from everyone else?*

- *What do you believe about your chances for outrageous success?*

- *What are you passionate about? When was a time that you were ecstatic?*

- *What action(s) would you take today if you had no chance of failure or unwanted repercussions?*

- *What would you do if you learned you had only a year to live? A day? An hour?*

- *To what are you committed above all else? Do your actions reflect that commitment?*

- *What are your wildest dreams? Are they really that wild?*

- *Of what did you dream as a child that you can now give yourself, in actuality or in essence?*

- *What is tethering you to the shore of a life that is less than you desire?*

- *Where would you really love to wake up tomorrow?*

- *What is your relationship with vulnerability? What about with personal power?*

- *In what physical stance do you feel most powerful? How can you be there more often?*

- *When was a time that you looked fear in the face and then moved right on through it?*

- *What desired experience, if never fulfilled, will you be sad on your deathbed to have missed?*

- *What would you do or say if you gave yourself permission to do or say anything?*

- *Where are you currently in comfortable inaction? Are you willing to take on the long-range risks and costs? For what are you willing to risk just about everything?*

Take a moment now to jot down any thoughts or ideas you'd like to capture here, and then dive on in. The water's fine!

_____

_____

_____

_____

_____

_____

_____

_____

_____

_____

_____

_____

_____

_____

_____

_____

_____

It takes courage to grow up and become who you really are. ~ e e cummings

Be You Out Loud.

The risk I intend to take today is:

_____

_____

_____

_____

_____

_____

The reason I will take this risk is:

_____

_____

_____

_____

_____

_____

_____

_____

_____

❑ I did it!   ❑ I didn't do it.

The rewards and/or lessons I received from taking (or not taking) the risk are:

_____

_____

_____

_____

_____

_____

_____

_____

_____

_____

_____

_____

_____

_____

_____

_____

_____

_____

_____

_____

_____

Twenty years from now you will be more disappointed by the things you didn't do than by the ones you did do. So throw off the bowlines. Sail away from the safe harbor. Catch the trade winds in your sails. Explore. Dream. Discover. ~ Mark Twain

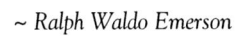

Always, always, always, always, always do what you are afraid to do.
~ *Ralph Waldo Emerson*

Be You Out Loud.

The risk I intend to take today is:

_____

_____

_____

_____

_____

_____

_____

The reason I will take this risk is:

_____

_____

_____

_____

_____

_____

_____

_____

_____

❑ I did it!   ❑ I didn't do it.

The rewards and/or lessons I received from taking (or not taking) the risk are:

_____

_____

_____

_____

_____

_____

_____

_____

_____

_____

_____

_____

_____

_____

_____

_____

_____

_____

_____

_____

_____

_____

_____

_____
_____
_____
_____
_____
_____
_____
_____
_____
_____
_____
_____
_____
_____
_____
_____
_____
_____
_____
_____
_____
_____
_____

We gain strength, and courage, and confidence by each experience in which we really stop to look fear in the face... we must do that which we think we cannot. ~ Eleanor Roosevelt

It is only by risking our persons from one hour to another that we live at all.

~ William James

Be You Out Loud.

The risk I intend to take today is:

_____

_____

_____

_____

_____

_____

The reason I will take this risk is:

_____

_____

_____

_____

_____

_____

_____

_____

❏ I did it!   ❏ I didn't do it.

The rewards and/or lessons I received from taking (or not taking) the risk are:

_____

_____

_____

_____

_____

_____

_____

_____

_____

_____

_____

_____

_____

_____

_____

_____

_____

_____

_____

_____

_There can be no vulnerability without risk; there can be
no community without vulnerability; there can be no peace,
and ultimately no life, without community._ ~ M. Scott Peck

The greatest mistake you can make in life is to be continually fearing you will make one. ~ Elbert Hubbard

18

Be You Out Loud.

The risk I intend to take today is:

_____

_____

_____

_____

_____

_____

The reason I will take this risk is:

_____

_____

_____

_____

_____

_____

_____

_____

_____

❑ I did it!   ❑ I didn't do it.

The rewards and/or lessons I received from taking (or not taking) the risk are:

_____

_____

_____

_____

_____

_____

_____

_____

_____

_____

_____

_____

_____

_____

_____

_____

_____

_____

_____

_____

_____

_____

I believe I'm here to speak my truth and that's all I have to do. I don't have to make people understand it… I just have to speak the truth. ~ Anne Wilson Schaef

Death is not the greatest loss in life. The greatest loss is what dies inside us while we live. ~ Norman Cousins

Be You Out Loud.

The risk I intend to take today is:

_____

_____

_____

_____

_____

_____

The reason I will take this risk is:

_____

_____

_____

_____

_____

_____

_____

_____

❑ I did it!   ❑ I didn't do it.

The rewards and/or lessons I received from taking (or not taking) the risk are:

_____

_____

_____

_____

_____

_____

_____

_____

_____

_____

_____

_____

_____

_____

_____

_____

_____

_____

_____

_____

_____

103

There are costs and risks to a program of action, but they are far less than the long-range risks and costs of comfortable inaction. ~ John F. Kennedy

Don't wait for the fear to leave before you take action — the action is what will eventually eliminate the fear. ~ John Sklare

Be You Out Loud.

The risk I intend to take today is:

_____

_____

_____

_____

_____

_____

The reason I will take this risk is:

_____

_____

_____

_____

_____

_____

_____

_____

❏ I did it!   ❏ I didn't do it.

The rewards and/or lessons I received from taking (or not taking) the risk are:

_____

_____

_____

_____

_____

_____

_____

_____

_____

_____

_____

_____

_____

_____

_____

_____

_____

_____

_____

_____

_____

_____

I've been absolutely terrified every moment of my life and I've never let it keep me from doing a single thing that I wanted to do. ~ Georgia O'Keefe

Avoiding danger is no safer in the long run than outright exposure. Life is either a daring adventure or nothing. ~ Helen Keller

21

Be You Out Loud.

LIVE

The risk I intend to take today is:

_____

_____

_____

_____

_____

_____

The reason I will take this risk is:

_____

_____

_____

_____

_____

_____

_____

_____

_____

❑ I did it!   ❑ I didn't do it.

The rewards and/or lessons I received from taking (or not taking) the risk are:

_____

_____

_____

_____

_____

_____

_____

_____

_____

_____

_____

_____

_____

_____

_____

_____

_____

_____

_____

_____

_____

_____

The paradox of courage is that a man must be a little careless of his life even in order to keep it. ~ G.K. Chesterton

Week Four: Lead

When I dare to be powerful – to use my strength in the service of my vision – then it becomes less and less important whether I am afraid. ~ Audre Lorde

Congratulations again – only one more week! You've been doing great, and now it's time to step it up once again and **Lead**!

Here are this week's questions to ponder:

- *What is your intention for your life?*

- *What do you hope for the individuals in your life? For our world as a whole?*

- *What impact are you having on those around you? What impact do you want to be having?*

- *When was the last time you asserted yourself for something you knew was right, whether or not it was popular?*

- *What social causes tug at your heart? Which ones do you support with your resources?*

- *What do you want others to say about you when you are gone? What do you want your legacy to be?*

- *What is your relationship with possibility? With limitlessness?*

- *Is there something happening in your community in which you feel called to get involved?*

- *What are you creating that no one else can or will?*

- *From what positions of leadership have you shied away in the past? Are they still available?*

- *What are your convictions?*

- *What do you believe about the reach of your influence?*

- *What is it that you have to say that is inspirational? Affirming? Empowering?*

- *What do you know to be true at the very core of you?*

- *When have you seen someone lead simply from living authentically?*

- *What would authentic life and leadership mean for you, personally?*

Take a moment now to jot down any thoughts or ideas you'd like to capture here, and then dive on in. The water's fine!

Once you choose hope, anything's possible.
~ Christopher Reeve

Be You Out Loud.

The risk I intend to take today is:

_____

_____

_____

_____

_____

_____

_____

The reason I will take this risk is:

_____

_____

_____

_____

_____

_____

_____

_____

_____

_____

_____

❏ I did it!   ❏ I didn't do it.

The rewards and/or lessons I received from taking (or not taking) the risk are:

_____

_____

_____

_____

_____

_____

_____

_____

_____

_____

_____

_____

_____

_____

_____

_____

_____

_____

_____

_____

_____

_____

_____

_____

_____

_____

_____

_____

_____

_____

_____

_____

_____

_____

_____

_____

_____

_____

_____

_____

_____

_____

_____

_____

_____

_____

_____

Life is "trying things to see if they work." - Ray Bradbury

Our visions begin with our desires.
~ Audre Lorde

Be You Out Loud.

L E A D

The risk I intend to take today is:

_____

_____

_____

_____

_____

_____

The reason I will take this risk is:

_____

_____

_____

_____

_____

_____

_____

_____

_____

❑ I did it!   ❑ I didn't do it.

The rewards and/or lessons I received from taking (or not taking) the risk are:

_____

_____

_____

_____

_____

_____

_____

_____

_____

_____

_____

_____

_____

_____

_____

_____

_____

_____

_____

_____

_____

_____

_____

_____
_____
_____
_____
_____
_____
_____
_____
_____
_____
_____
_____
_____
_____
_____
_____
_____
_____
_____
_____
_____

Become a possibilitarian. No matter how dark things seem to be or actually are, raise your sights and see possibilities – always see them, for they're always there.

~ Norman Vincent Peale

What makes you a leader is having the courage of your convictions. ~ Queen Latifah

Be You Out Loud.

The risk I intend to take today is:

_____

_____

_____

_____

_____

_____

_____

The reason I will take this risk is:

_____

_____

_____

_____

_____

_____

_____

_____

_____

LEAD

❑ I did it!   ❑ I didn't do it.

The rewards and/or lessons I received from taking (or not taking) the risk are:

_____

_____

_____

_____

_____

_____

_____

_____

_____

_____

_____

_____

_____

_____

_____

_____

_____

_____

_____

Deep Democracy is our sense that the world is here to help us to become our entire selves, and that we are here to help the world to become whole. ~ Arnold Mindell

Only those who dare to fail greatly can ever achieve greatly. ~ Robert F. Kennedy

Be You Out Loud.

The risk I intend to take today is:

_____

_____

_____

_____

_____

_____

The reason I will take this risk is:

_____

_____

_____

_____

_____

_____

_____

_____

_____

_____

❑ I did it!   ❑ I didn't do it.

The rewards and/or lessons I received from taking (or not taking) the risk are:

_____

_____

_____

_____

_____

_____

_____

_____

_____

_____

_____

_____

_____

_____

_____

_____

_____

_____

_____

_____

_____

_____

_____

_____

Courage doesn't always roar. Sometimes courage is the quiet voice at the end of the day saying, "I will try again tomorrow." ~ Mary Ann Radmacher

...if we do not change our daily lives, we cannot change the world. ~ Thich Nhat Hanh

Be You Out Loud.

LEAD

The risk I intend to take today is:

_____

_____

_____

_____

_____

_____

_____

The reason I will take this risk is:

_____

_____

_____

_____

_____

_____

_____

_____

_____

❑ I did it!   ❑ I didn't do it.

The rewards and/or lessons I received from taking (or not taking) the risk are:

_____

_____

_____

_____

_____

_____

_____

_____

_____

_____

_____

_____

_____

_____

_____

_____

_____

_____

_____

_____

_____

_____

_____

_____

_____

The truth of the matter is that you always know the right thing to do. The hard part is doing it.

~ H. Norman Schwarzkopf

If your actions inspire others to dream more, learn more, do more and become more, you are a leader. ~ John Quincy Adams

Be You Out Loud.

The risk I intend to take today is:

_____

_____

_____

_____

_____

_____

The reason I will take this risk is:

_____

_____

_____

_____

_____

_____

_____

_____

_____

_____

❏ I did it!   ❏ I didn't do it.

The rewards and/or lessons I received from taking (or not taking) the risk are:

_____

_____

_____

_____

_____

_____

_____

_____

_____

_____

_____

_____

_____

_____

_____

_____

_____

_____

_____

_____

_____

_____

_____

_____

_____

_____

_____

_____

_____

_____

_____

_____

_____

_____

_____

_____

_____

_____

_____

_____

_____

_____

_____

_____

_____

A leader is one who knows the way, goes the way, and shows the way. ~ John C. Maxwell

The greatest glory in living lies not in never falling, but in rising every time we fall.

~ Nelson Mandela

Be You Out Loud.

LEAD

The risk I intend to take today is:

_____

_____

_____

_____

_____

_____

The reason I will take this risk is:

_____

_____

_____

_____

_____

_____

_____

_____

_____

❑ I did it!   ❑ I didn't do it.

The rewards and/or lessons I received from taking (or not taking) the risk are:

_____

_____

_____

_____

_____

_____

_____

_____

_____

_____

_____

_____

_____

_____

_____

_____

_____

_____

_____

_____

_____

_____

_____

Courage is contagious. When a brave man takes a stand, the spines of others are stiffened. ~ Billy Graham

Congratulations, Thank You and a Request

A final and great big congratulations to you!

Thank you, also, for all that you have put into this process. I am happy that you have done this for yourself and grateful that you have done it for our world! I know that you are on your way to **Learning, Loving, Living** and **Leading** in an even more authentic way than before, and that this is the beginning of something grand for you...

Please do send me a note, if you feel so inclined – let me know what the process was like for you, and where you are headed now as a result. You can most easily reach me via email at **Laura@TrueVoices.com.** I look forward to hearing from you very soon!

The Beginning!

If you don't risk anything,
you risk even more.

~ Erica Jong

Appendix I
111 Examples of Risks I've Taken

APPENDIX I: *111* Examples of Risks I've Taken

1. Asked for help

2. Asked lots of questions

3. Asked the mayor out for coffee

4. Attended networking events where I knew no one

5. Auditioned lots and lots of times

6. Became an entrepreneur

7. Believed in myself

8. Called potential clients and asked for the business

9. Changed my mind

10. Conducted interviews with famous people

11. Danced in public

12. Dealt with debt

13. Designed and taught classes, teleclasses

14. Did lots of things I'd never done before

15. Disclosed private things to friends

16. Discussed difficult topics

17. Divorced my husband, a lovely man with whom I was not in love

18. Drew and painted without any training

19. Drove on the freeway

20. Exhibited and sold some of my original art

21. Expressed my dissatisfaction with certain situations

22. Expressed my unhappiness at having received poor customer service

23. Gave a revealing personal interview for an article in a national magazine

24. Gave an hour-long impromptu speech

25. Gave myself permission to share my sexual orientation

26. Gave scripted speeches

27. Got a coach

28. Got mammograms

29. Got a perm

30. Got into the deep end of the pool

31. Got married

32. Got on a boat in a storm

33. Got on stage and sang with a favorite performer

34. Got plants that I knew I might kill

35. Had gratitude for my body

36. Had my poetry published

37. Hired assistants; let go of assistants

38. Hired a cleaning service

39. Jumped into the pool of social media

40. Learned to drive

41. Learned to drive a stick shift

42. Led book studies

43. Let fear hold me back

44. Left several business partnerships that were no longer a fit

45. Left Houston

46. Let a friend go

47. Listened to my gut

48. Looked in the mirror and said "I love you."

49. Made difficult choices

50. Made unhealthy choices

51. Meditated

52. Ordered furniture without knowing whether or not it would work

53. Performed a "Shitty First Draft" of my one-woman show

54. Performed in the 12-grade talent show, while in 3rd grade (and won!)

55. Played the UnGame

56. Posed nude / modeled for life drawing classes

57. Posed nude / modeled for photography project, had my picture (without my face) in exhibits and a national magazine

58. Posed nude / modeled for sculpting classes

59. Pushed myself physically

60. Put myself in treatment for an eating disorder

61. Quit my job (and salary)

62. Raised my rates, raised them again

63. Read my poetry aloud

64. Reconnected with friends from way back

65. Refused to be treated poorly

66. *Rescued two dogs of "dangerous breeds"*

67. *Resigned from a non-profit board that was no longer right for me*

68. *Returned calls*

69. *Said "I don't know."*

70. *Said "I love you."*

71. *Said "maybe"*

72. *Said "no"*

73. *Said "yes"*

74. *Sang and acted in front of thousands of people*

75. *Sang karaoke badly*

76. *Sent birthday cards and gifts even though they were belated*

77. *Set boundaries*

78. *Showed my photography at an arts fair*

79. *Showed my enthusiasm*

80. *Signed up for coach training*

81. *Smoked a total of two cigarettes*

82. *Sold my silver and my leather coat for cash*

83. *Spent all my money*

84. *Spent time in my hammock*

85. *Spoke up about my desire for things to change*

86. *Stated my preferences*

87. *Stayed on my food plan*

88. *Stayed true to myself*

89. Stayed when the scared part of me wanted to run

90. Talked to neighbors about a situation on our street concerning dog neglect

91. Told the truth

92. Took a "red tent" day

93. Took a leave of absence from school before finishing my degrees

94. Took care of my dying father

95. Took classes in subjects I found intimidating

96. Took out ads

97. Took the afternoon off and went to a movie

98. Traveled to countries where I didn't know the language

99. Tried foods I'd never eaten

100. Trusted

101. Walked away from business that was not a fit for me

102. Walked barefooted

103. Walked past angry people with shotguns

104. Went for it

105. Went on and off my medicine

106. Went swimming

107. Went to therapy

108. Worried

109. Wrote my morning pages every day (except for the days I didn't)

110. Wrote this book, knowing that I'll want to change it immediately after publishing it

111. Wrote this list for you to see and read

Appendix II
Some Other Books for You

APPENDIX II: Some Other Books for You

Below is a list of books that you may want to explore as you continue to deepen your relationship with risk-taking. I'm sure that there are many other great resources, as well, but these will be a good start, and among them are some books I've read many times and love dearly. I wish the same for you.

Be Full of Yourself: The Journey from Self-Criticism to Self-Celebration
written by Patricia Lynn Reilly

Bird by Bird: Some Instructions on Writing and Life
written by Anne Lamott

Feel the Fear and Do It Anyway
written by Susan Jeffers

Fierce Conversations: Achieving Success at Work and in Life One Conversation at a Time
written by Susan Scott

Find Your Courage: 12 Acts for Becoming Fearless at Work and in Life
written by Margie Warrell

I Will Not Die an Unlived Life
written by Dawna Markova

Positive Risk: How Smart Women Use Passion
to Break Through Their Fears
written by Barbara Stoker

Right Risk: 10 Powerful Principles for
Taking Giant Leaps with Your Life
written by Bill Treasurer

risk, courage, and women:
contemporary voices in prose and poetry,
edited by Karen A. Waldron, Laura M. Labatt and Janice H. Brazil

The Artist's Way: A Spiritual Path to Higher Creativity
written by Julia Cameron, with Mark Bryan

The Dance of Deception: A Guide to Authenticity
and Truth-Telling in Women's Relationships
written by Harriet Learner

The Invitation
written by Oriah Mountain Dreamer

The Third Chapter: Passion, Risk, and Adventure
in the 25 Years After 50
written by Sara Lawrence-Lightfoot

What Would You Do If You Had No Fear
written by Diane Conway

Acknowledgments

In addition to my own personal and professional experiences, this program is chock full of ideas and concepts that came to me through my involvement with other people, programs, media and/or organizations. Without these influences, and the people who have supported my work along the way, these ideas would never have been formulated and this book would not exist.

Therefore, I wish to thank the following:

- *Anita Horsley*
- *Anita Johnston, PhD*
- *Anne Lamott*
- *Aviva Jane Carlin*
- *Barbara McAfee*
- *BevAnn Bonds*
- *Bill Floyd, Mayor of Decatur, GA*
- *Byron Katie*
- *Carolyn Cook*
- *Charis Books and More*
- *Charlotte Kasl, PhD*
- *Claudia Brogan*
- *Claudia Crenshaw, RN, PhD*
- *Coaches Training Institute*
- *Concept Synergy*
- *Cynthia Loy Darst, MCC*
- *Daniel Ladinsky*
- *David Whyte*
- *Dawna Wade*
- *Debbie Kerr*
- *Debby Stone, JD, PCC*
- *Essie Escobedo*
- *Eva Gregory, MCC*
- *Jana Stanfield*
- *Janie Cook*
- *Jeanine Mancusi, MCC*
- *John Brasher*
- *Julia Cameron*
- *Karen Drucker*
- *Kathleen Falvey Brown*
- *Kathy Muns*
- *Kendra and Jeff Armacost*
- *Lee Glickstein*
- *Leza Danly, MCC*
- *Lisa Hinely*

- *Lisa Michaels*
- *Lori Buff*
- *Louise L. Hay*
- *Madonna Ministry*
- *Marcy Nelson-Garrison, MA, CPCC*
- *Marianne Williamson*
- *Marita Fridjhon, MSW, ORSCC and Faith Fuller, PhD, ORSCC*
- *Mark Bryan*
- *Mary Oliver*
- *My dear Speaking Circle Peer Group (Betsy P., Bill C., Denise W., Elizabeth M., Joanne S. L., Kim F., Kris D., Lisa L., Martha C., Martha E., Stacey M., Wendy W.)*
- *My P.I.N.K. Paradigm Community*
- *My gorgeous Lucid Living family*
- *Nanci Griffith*
- *Naomi Shihab Nye*

- *Oprah Winfrey*
- *Oriah Mountain Dreamer*
- *Patricia Lynn Reilly*
- *R. Michael Prudent, MD*
- *Rita Balzotti*
- *Roger Housden*
- *Sarah Snow, in loving memory*
- *Sary Korrick Newman*
- *Sue Monk Kidd*
- *Susan Warren*
- *Suzanne Bird-Harris*
- *Suzanne Sterling*
- *The Beautiful Blogging Babes of RiskADay.com*
- *The incredible interviewees in my next book,* Conversations with True Voices
- *The lovely and talented book designer, whose beautiful work you are now viewing, Vanessa Lowry.*

And most especially, I wish to thank the following:

My parents, Mary Ann and Jim Taylor, and Robert Overstreet – Your love, support, acceptance, patience, and encouragement have been, and still are, immeasurable. My hope is that one day you will know the depth of my gratitude for the gifts you have given me – gifts of both nature and nurture.

My clients and students, current and past – You inspire and teach me more than you'll ever know. The fact that you entrust your hearts and dreams to me is an honor I hold dear and will never take lightly.

My (four-legged) children and their (two-legged) dad, Jasper Biering, Tucker Biering, Dogberry Overstreet Biering, Little Bit Biering and Mark Biering, respectively – The ways you have loved me will never cease to amaze and uplift me.

My sweetheart, Martha Carnahan – The way you see the "me" I am inside, and the "me" that I could become, while having such "gentle disregard" for the parts of me that I can have a hard time seeing past, blows my mind. Your presence in my life is a gift beyond compare. You are a gift beyond compare, and one that I will cherish always.

And to those whose names have been inadvertently excluded, I thank you, too!

If you have crossed my path,
you have had an impact on me and on my life.

Whether or not you are listed here, please know that
I am grateful for our encounter(s)
and I look forward to crossing paths again soon.

www.TheRiskADayJournal.com

About the Author

Laura Overstreet Biering, MM, CPCC, PCC

Your Authentic Life and Leadership Coach

Laura Biering has been told that she has an "infectious zeal" for taking daily risks and for coaching people who want to do enlivening work and live inspired lives. She works with individuals, partners and teams who are ready for radical, authentic success – success their way! Her clients learn to take risks from the heart – both big and small – in order to reach their goals and dreams, and create realities that rock.

Now a veteran of the coaching profession, Laura brings a wealth of additional experience through her varied work history. Her stops along the way to coaching have included the following: bank teller, opera singer, legal recruiter and giant pickle (yes, you read that correctly). In addition, she is an Ordained Interfaith Minister, and still performs the occasional ceremony. As you might imagine from the variety of her past endeavors and interests, her client list is just as varied.

In addition to her experience, skills and training, Laura brings warm compassion, wild creativity and an unexpectedly wicked sense of humor to all that she does. She is deeply committed to Authentic Learning, Loving, Living and Leading, and enjoys retreating on her SE Georgia farm with her partner and their adorable, four-legged children.

Laura would love to be visited at **www.TrueVoices.com, www.RiskADay.com** and **www.BrinsonsRace.com**. You may also contact her directly via email at **Laura@TrueVoices.com**.

Should you be someone who prefers a more formal approach to Laura's qualifications, on the next page are two lists for you!

Education:

- *Professional Certified Coach, as designated by the International Coach Federation*
- *Graduate, Organization and Relationship Systems Coach Training, Center for Right Relationship*
- *Authorized Facilitator, Team Diagnostic Assessment, Team Coaching International*
- *Graduate, Team Coaching Intensive, Team Coaching International*
- *Graduate, Lucid Living Program*
- *Certified Strategic Attraction Coach, Perfect Customers, Inc.*
- *Certified Co-Active Coach, The Coaches Training Institute*
- *Ordained Interfaith Minister, Madonna Ministry*
- *Certified Facilitator, The Artist's Way at Work*
- *Certified Facilitator, Expressive Dance, Awakening to the Divine Feminine; Graduate of the Priestess Process, The Institute of Conscious Expression*
- *Certified Paralegal, with honors, National Center for Paralegal Training (ABA accredited)*
- *Bachelor and Master of Music (Vocal Performance), Rice University*

Affiliations:

- *True Voices, Inc., founder, CEO*
- *Corner Office Coaching, co-founder, Chief Creative Officer*
- *Georgia Coach Association, active member, past board member*
- *International Coach Federation, active member, past committee member*
- *The Complete Lawyer e-zine, former senior editor and contributing author*
- *ProWIN (Professional Women's Information Network), active lifetime member, committee co-chair*
- *Decatur Business Association of Decatur, GA, active member*
- *Be You Out Loud™ program and associated products, creator and facilitator*
- *LoveDesigned℠ and PartnershipDesigned℠, co-creator and facilitator*
- *A Guide to Getting It: Sacred Healing, contributing author*
- *Love your Body, Live your Life℠ program and associated products, creator and facilitator*
- *Organic Networking℠ program, co-creator and facilitator*